CAROLINE CLARK

Saying Yes in Russian

AGENDA EDITIONS

ISBN 978-1-908527-04-2

First published in 2012 by Agenda Editions,
The Wheelwrights, Fletching Street,
Mayfield, East Sussex TN20 6TL

Printed and bound in Great Britain

Acknowledgements to the editors of the following journals: *Agenda, The Frogmore Papers, The Interpreter's House, The Malahat Review, The North, PN Review, Poetry Review, Smiths Knoll.*

Thanks to the Canada Council for the Arts for a grant to attend a poetry workshop at the Sage Hill Writing Experience.

I would also like to thank Andrei, my parents, Clare, Kelda, Kelly, Ksenia, Marcus, Nebojša, Irina, O.A. and Patricia McCarthy. A special thanks to the Russian department of Exeter University during 1995-1999.

Caroline Clark has been a chosen young Broadsheet poet and essayist in past issues of *Agenda*. She studied German and Russian at Exeter University and upon graduation in 1999 moved to Moscow, where she lived until 2007. During that time she returned to the UK for a year to complete an MA in Modern European Literature at Sussex University, where she wrote her dissertation on Paul Celan and Osip Mandelstam.

She comes from Lewes in Sussex and now lives in Montreal where she is currently translating work by the Russian poet Olga Sedakova.

CONTENTS

I

Saying Yes in Russian

To Andrei

Morning

Night Train

Ahead
the untouched tracks

become
the foregone night

we pass ourselves in fleeting images
void becoming lightened window

becoming void becoming thought:
perhaps there lies the Russia of our dreams

we shuttle through past roots and bark
beyond the forest's blackened wood.

Tale

And then I came to a place
where the tower blocks stop
and do not give way to woods
or open field. They end in the edge
of their ending. They stop.

I had set off like many before
in autumn. Underfoot a mishmash
of leaves. First came potholes,
things to avoid, obscenities.
Or was it gestures – a tugging

at comprehension? First came the word.
They took me to a village wedding,
the name of the place meant apple.
Yábloko, yábloko. Give me a word
I can understand. Say it with a bite.

Apples, Russian apples, the year's
late harvest remembered. Buy
a bucket of my finest, ever so
sour, the best. And here's a sprig
of flowering dill, just for you.

Here is only memory giving up
its silence. Later alone come crunching
through snow, come in from the cold with frost
on your clothes smelling of yellowing
apples. These words are not my own.

A is for apple, *ya* is for *yábloko.*
The jaw, the cheek, where both
can meet. Difference a place between
tongue and teeth. Say it with a bite.
Say it until you get it right.

Zdravstvuite

Hello is the hardest word to say
in Russian, beginners find. She puts up
the biggest hurdles at the start. Leap now
from word to phrase, request to heart-to-heart.
If you really want me, come at me running,
we might hear her say. Whispers come later,
a walk in her white wood alone.

It's wider there in Russia

or rawer, corruption or
tastelessness more barefaced.
Take the trip of a decade
but the litter shows we're
all from the same world.
One took the high road. Still,
the state of things to come
can't possibly be judged.
Horror hard to run towards.
Nights out are barer, more
grisly. The blind-eyeing of
destitute Moscow. This dark
night scrambling to get in, get
out. Morning vodka breath.
Metro rush. Winter sweat.

Red Square

A thousand or so metres above sea level,
an island unto itself

following the curvature of the earth,
cobbled and set with pearls.

Traded on, celebrated on, betrayed on,
promises made on, enslaved on,
displayed, prayed, paraded on,
over, across and down to the Moscow River,
world's waterway, with a flash of coat-tails, skirts, heels, gone.

Rigged by four masts to the centre of the globe
it sails out on a home-wind.
Deep as the century,
what it has lost is buried there,
was never there.

Moscow Honey Fair

May, acacia, rosebay willow herb, sage,
white clover, wild strawberry, taiga,
linden, forest, clover, meadow, pollen,
holy clover, hawthorn, coriander, pumpkin,
garden angelica, raspberry, spring garden,
honeydew, buckwheat, cedar, milkweed,
mountain ash, blackcurrant, sunflower,
mignonette, blackberry, chestnut.

Tatarstan, Tyan-Shan, Kazakhstan,
Adigei, Altai, Tambov, Kirov, Rostov,
Voronezh, Jewish Autonomous District,
Perm, Kursk, Far East, Lipetsk, Kemerovo,
Kraznodar, Volgograd, the Volga, Oryol,
Chuvashiya, Mordovia, Kyrgizia, Bashkiria,
Alania, North Ossetia, Chechnya.

Oasis

Smells rise. The old snow is turned and bulldozed
into heaps that fade and stain the pre-spring days.
Heads are lighter now. Around us buildings rise
and fall. Out there the snow melts from the centre
out. An oasis of sodden earth, a faded remembering
of grass. Shifting rooftops shed their loads. Bluetits
tinker springnotes, chinking crystal through cigarette
snow. We breathe a sea-thawed air from a sea
that isn't there. Weightlessness takes the strain.

Two Words

First you taught me *protálina*,
where earth laid bare
through melting snow
becomes a circle of spring.
There the street dog basks on
last year's grass, warming newly.

Later I mouthed to memory
another: *opúshka*. Where
the forest finally finds its end.
I hear a rush of fir trees as
someone pushes through,
entering meadowed light.

Of all those words whose
shaded paths I've walked,
I find these two growing side
by side, sisters in their lilting land,
whispering tales of places
once unknown, unnamed.

See them step from their
swaying pine and birchwood
sea into warm daylight. How
delicately they wear their names:
Protálina and Opúshka,
the story of a struggle at its end.

Dark Blue Line, North-East

From Izmailovsky Park to
Izmailovskaya you shoot above
ground. One side: the red brick clock
tower and depot, old forgotten wagons, on
the other: grand hunting grounds, the tallest silver
birches, woodpeckers echoing above holiday
crowds. Then on to white highrise lives.
Identical carpets, cutlery, chairs, ahead –
multitudinous life.

Malchik of the Scrapheap

Malchik's in the scrapheap at the back
of building three, rooting round for treasures
but what about me? I'm going around the block,
a thousand miles away, noting down the number
plates of parked and passing cars. Malchik's way
ahead, sorting through his finds – a tv tube to smash
or drop from balcony four, deodorant cans to throw
exploding into fires, a photo to keep, a coin to keep,
an album of hockey players to keep. I'm conquering
my street, mapping out the water-points sunk into
the ground, tallying up all the trees I can get my
arms around and signposts I can reach.

About now Malchik,
you'll be watching your first tv ad and sketch
it lovingly in class. Befriend the water-melon
seller, assist him free of charge. You'll wait two
hours for a Big Mac next to Pushkin Square (take
one home by train, divide it into four). With your
friends you'll walk for miles on bread and fizzy
drink. Now stop to paint graveyard scenes along
a railway fence. I'm still going around the block. At
night I look inside my jewellery box, admire the velvet
blue. Watch the ballerina twirling on her lake. Behind
her stands a swan. You're Malchik of the scrapheap
and I'm lady of the lake, soothsayer of these parts.
Fear not, I'll find my way, but take care, it's you
who must find me. Ready now, one two three.

Malchik and his 3-D Slides

There's something of a Fellini ragamuffin
about them all, street urchin looks and poses.
'Hold still', he takes one shot, 'don't move',
and rocks onto the other leg to take the second
shot. Sliva never got it quite right, his face a
double-take blur. I peer in at them against this
lamp light. Each leaf, the clumps of grass around
their feet. Balanced on railway sleepers. Rubble,
puddles that you can step inside. I can almost
see behind them. Zhmursky who got meningitis.
He'd never had any hair – at least not until he
was twelve (what was it like) black and very fine.
There's Oleg who fancied fat girls. He could work
a National Geographic picture. And Vovich who
died of cancer. Kustodiev's Venus any day.

I switch to a silent view, Malchik's view from
Malchik's balcony, watching Malchik's sunset.
'I had to do something, couldn't just leave it in
peace'. I'll watch it with you. That bird. Fencelife.

Malchik Smells the West

Malchik's on his patch, one slab
of concrete on Old Arbat Street.
Today the tourists have come,
touting their brands from the West.
Malchik says yes to one Texas is
Best t-shirt (swapped for one Lenin's
head) and one Bazooka Joe baseball
cap (for one Budyonovka hat). At
home he puts away the clothes,
breathing in their scent. Such fragrant
foreignness. A smell he'd like to own.

The future is fresh with Ariel, Persil,
Pearl and Tide, heralds of a change.
Not quite flowers in a meadow or
a stretch of alpine ice, rather a synth-
icated sweetness, the freshly laundered
west. The future's right beside him –
now ahead, now behind – it rises up to
greet him, seemingly at home in his
wardrobe and drawers, seemingly his own.

At Play

I was Stalin, he was Beria,
Pasha was Mandelstam.
'Well, Tovarish Stalin?'
'Repress him, Tovarish Beria!'
And Ilia bashed Pasha
over the head with a book.

New Shaving Brush, c.1999

He holds it aloft
in the kitchen:
'It looks pre-Revolution
or Italian, like something
from the Mediterranean'.
'Sherlock Holmes?' I suggest.
'No Soviet rubbish,
that's for sure'.

'What was it like?'
'An okay place. A mad house'.
From here all I see –
long brown corridors,
sheets of glass you can only
project your voice towards.

Tell me,

I say, the sounds
you used to love. But before
you can, I give mine.
The slanting rain on wild black nights,
me inside below it dry.
The heating coming on,
its clicking comfort
promising maybe a frost, maybe snow,
maybe that the world will be changed.

For you,
a summer evening,
the kind you used to get.
The balcony door open
and Dad watching football inside.
Sounds mix,
the distant cries of kids,
the late light evenings carrying over
in their shouts.
That world was enough, you say.

The Poplars

We've taken to yard walking,
watch the lights come on, sit on swings.
The poplars are tired-dry now, but even
back in spring we knew what they'd become.
For a few nights after returning
we manage to sleep without protest.
The weather has dulled our senses,
the yard guitar quietened since summer.

Early still, when the first dog barks,
you talk of finding another place,
a third country, neither yours nor mine.
I turn in protest, watch the morning
flicker across the floor. The poplars
have their say, turning sunslants into
windowed waterlight. Someday we'll be living
these turns of phrases, blank unknown spaces.

Years later, when walking up foreign stairs,
will I stop and sit in protest?
How many choices will I have seen
ripen and fall? Perhaps I'll whisper back
you could never have tasted them all.
And will you and I share the same vowels,
the same nostalgia for fresh-leafed poplars
quenching these morning yards?

Like Notes Playing on a Harp

Like notes playing on a harp, this clear April morning.
The sun warms a shoulder, and the trees in every square,
just like Jewish elders at the start of Passover
with blue-black beards on show, must be delightful now.
Light falls on the wall, table and sheets of paper.
Light is a shadow bestowed to us by an angel.
All other things come later: garden dragonflies, glory –
how serene the church domes must be, tapering
into this clear morning, morning becoming midday,
morning like a harp and like what else? I forget.

Translation of '*Вроде игры на арфе чистое утро апреля*'
by Leonid Aronzon

Siesta

Before home

road comes to a tree tunnel stretch of darkness,
enter alone.
Field lies black to the left
and beyond is everything brought to these parts
by dreams, regret.
Overhead flits moon.
See her now through the branches.
Scamperings by the roadside
soon, soon.

Morandi's Siesta

Noon arrives on Via Fondazza, siesta
lulls the shuttered air with rosemary, pine,
melon skin, rind, pockets of thyme. It crests a

wave across earth-worn streets and skyline
to find him caught inside the midday maze
of absence. He watches a bottle of wine,

vases, jugs and jars. A cool wall, the haze
of dust. Stark sunlight. Shapes stir then emerge
as still life caught mid-life founders in his gaze.

One touches the edge of another, lines merge
with seeming intent, blossoming lives of their own.
Attention unfurls as a flower and traces the curve

of a petal-thin rim upwards and out, now roams
through distant valleys. Likenesses flourish and wane,
saying never alone, no one is ever alone,

and never the same, nothing is ever the same
twice over. The tree outside his window
presses its weight against the milky pane,

heavy with human softness. Long hollow
in his corner bed, he watches figures meet;
the people that are never there follow

on in pairs and trios. Conceit, intrigue, defeat
and death. A cluster of three takes the floor,
retreats. Conceals their secret centre. Repeat...

as siesta tugs him away from shore
he whispers, I know these things, am these things,
then signs his name, pleased but wanting more.

Storm Trawling

Darkened life we wait
(the thick lick of raindrops
concrete pink, blackened earth)

to plunder a line of ants.
Asphalt pounded to pungent pine,
urgent tastes this life.

Now is the rush to find
the drunk-drowned bits
of lost, emerging, predatory life:

hand dip and trawl
seaweed, shred-wood
for sea-slung beauties
dredged up heavy from their bed.

O come for staggered crabs,
blunt-ended seaslugs
gory in their reactionless state,

tossed medusa fish
held through dripping fingers –
all tideborne gifts of the day.

Come you passing beachwalkers,
bring your nods, your jealous eyes
to treasures here holed up on shore.

Who sits now waiting still
to starve and plunder,
who knows what glory,
what wastes will come?

The Presence of Sunlight

Early morning. A street sets up
the distance. A distance I can see,
though veiled with hope, wild
incalculable things. At the end,
a pink haze. I move in the cool
air of a day yet to grow hot. It's
a future there. Like a season past
you can't believe in now it's gone.
An abandon remains. You pass
tulips, things of summer,
the humid air of a promised day.

Years later this abandon remains.
There are no people. But in
this peopleless state everything is
done for you. Think back to that
hazy summer street. Only now
the presence of sunlight is all
there is. A moment of memoried
light. And it returns, returns, returns
to you until you take it up in your
thoughts. You, the beacon it has
been seeking out. Look at it, say
what have we here?

Evening

Swifts

I watch
evening swifts
dip
pivot on
impulses
like lightfall
sensing no space
no sky or earth
they rise by flank
and fall to cusp kokoshniki
tracing wing-tipped bliss
round late lit cupola

these star-lit cupola
tethered in reverence,
kissed and set in place
to receive, relinquish light,
now fullbodied
    now eclipsed.

Now Free from Weighty Notes

Now free from weighty notes
and the draft you've thrown away,
a single phrase held fast
inside the mind's dark space.
Eyes shut, it's holding tight,
propelled by self alone,
from paper see it rise –
a spire to empty skies.

Translation of 'Octet No. 6' ('*Когда, уничтожив набросок*')
by Osip Mandelstam

Translation Query

No word for *resent* in Russian,
you must take another route –
indignant, offended, hurt.
Inflated, shrinking, shrunk.
Resent – a tent built right up
out from you. Inside, cathedral,
firmament, night. Camera obscura,
pinhole of the mind. Never said,
never did, should have known. Memory
winds its way until the meaning's all
your own. Twisted root. An inward
growing rose that blooms for you alone.
Speak now or forever hold its thorn.

Snowfall

Tram cables
settle neatly in peaks
      spray newly
to recover in freshfall.

Silently it slips
  from statues' laps and shoulders
softening the blow.

We trace our tracks
    lightest footfall
ever known.

May the Earth

In this country I learn
to say *praise be to God* for
relief of any magnitude and
may the earth be feather-soft
for him at times of formal grief.
I learn to mean it later. There we
stand by his grave, cold March,
thankful for the blue sky, crisp
ground, praying he will rest as if
on a bed of softest duckdown.

Sea Shanty

O life in the dative case
is the only one for me,
tacking against a headwind,
sailing out to sea.

Keep your nominative perfection
set on distant shores,
no completion or arrival,
may I always be headed towards.

O life in the dative case
is the only one for me,
sculpted by direction,
that's the only way to be.

To Tula

Last year we went to Tula
to Tula we went last year,
we walked the streets of Tula
to see what we could find:
the kremlin, armoury chamber,
a crafted horseshoed flea,
gingerbread presses, sugar tongs,
all manner of pots for tea.
For we had gone to Tula
to note for what she was known,
yet I remember Tula
for two lilac trees alone,
one white, one lilac like the name,
above a sky-starred cupola
and a mist of scented rain.
We took the train from Tula
from Tula we took the train,
for we had been to Tula
and we hope she was glad we came.

May Day at Sokolniki

Toilets in the park, a saucer for
your coins, plastic plants. A doily.
Rag to wipe your boots on. Come
summer they'll yank the hot water tap
off. Bars on ground floor windows. White
curtains softening the sunlight. Women
drinking tea, plastic bags covering
their shoes. Clean. It's coming in
behind them. White and dust-laden,
old light. The type there used to be.

Dacha

i

They wait
in white expectation

a tablecloth
tatters in the sun

minutes long gone
circle like flies

and still the blank-eyed days
push on through the taiga.

ii

Mosquitoes descend
at twilight

cups accumulate
saying when

hours tag
the stork's crooked flight

and the rocking chair
deepens its grooves
trying, trying to remember.

iii

Absent visitors
long gone

a cloth
tatters

they wait
in white

memories
circle

Beyond the Horizon, Steppe, Blue Fence

Now take this map
and find where no straight streets are.
Walk along the highway,
gradient on the rise,
naked retreat of snow,
flint-grey concrete
warm enough to warm yourself on,
yellow-gas horizon gesturing on
to the steppe beyond.

Now turn off
into the end of what you know:
here hole opened long ago,
ruin too far gone to photograph.
Here timber, izba, samovar, terror
that there'd be no other place to go,
underfoot no trace
of what came before,
land scraped raw.

O visitor flail for beauty,
no faded homeliness here,
anything you see is gone.
Here rise new towers,
fortressed safe.
Below grows lilac old style
behind a blue fence.
Here stands a new sign
– Centre –
for what is a place
without one?

Drive North

into warm white nights
where the river holds
its light past midnight

watch with mothers by the shore
their children's silhouettes
taking dips in violet waters

wait – you'll never see
yourself grow old

here differences dawn lightly,
first away, then towards.

At Yasnaya Polyana

Come to a rafter
within the stable's cool,
two silk-sooted swallows
above a horse at rest.

Who knows such tail-tipped balance
unthought, untrained?
Lástochka, lástochka,
loved first then named.

Inside

What's inside this local sounding
hall? Lozenges to swish around,
push outside. No hidden coves
or tongue-tucked tides. But sky.
A plain palated wide. Cornflower
blue. See a flower, pick it. A house,
knock three times. Wait, then enter.
Here agony, there translucent
delight. Outside, a silver birch
       revelling in the breeze.

The Desert and the Nightingale

For Moscow

i

The Myth of the Desert

Round they circle like a desert rose battered
by centuries' sand, nowhere left to go.
All that you've heard, nothing you've heard is real.
You can grind all myths to dust. Having always
been there, they had never arrived; having
never arrived they had never been there.
You can walk these streets to dust, place
of no arrivals, direction laid to rest.

Here in the city that's never there, head deeper.
You can grind all myths to dust till there's nothing
left to know. You can walk these streets to bone,
circle broken torsos till the centre
wears you down. Nothing you've heard is real.
You've never been there. Through sand, seek water.

The Myth of the Nightingale

Arrowshadowed I wait at the city's core,
earthbound in dust. First murmurs an underground
stream, gurgling audible waterways, sound
becoming beaded globes propelled through narrow
canals. When away is all I know – now break
these ambersounded notes. All of me is burgeoning
to burst these boulders, pebbles and stones and over-
flow, flower into the kerbside world.

All that you hear is real. May you be blessed
in strangeness, loved in newness. I'll shake you loose
a summer storm against the background roar.
Through jasmine and lime, I'll sing you to my source.
Let there be flowers in the sand, lilacs in the streets.
I can make more life, more life than the sun.

Tonight Moscow

when your streets are beyond
the touch of sun
and darkness gulfs your greying gullies
let your rooftops flare red
flank by flank
each stand of white

from shadow streets to desert fire,
your heights to where the railway track
cuts through a depth now filled with light,
one second acres wide
set with stones of paradise –
Moscow, flare red
tonight.

Saying Yes in Russian

Place the tip of your tongue
against the roof of your mouth
pressing the point just behind your teeth.
Push up, jaw tough, eyes hard.
Make as if to say *no, nyet,*
think of the negative *n* of never, at least, not yet.
In this position and state of mind,
swiftly release the tongue forward and down;
you must surprise it, yourself and the one who asked.
Then turn that heavy knock of a *n*
into the delicate etiquette of *da.*

II

Done, in Gold

To Greta

What Is the Word –

What is the word for this
in French? The Russian I know –
a kind of chucking out. Brutal,
gets to the point though. The English
applies restraint. A thing mislaid,
mistake. A stately horsedrawn flourish.
Miscarriage, o, how ravishingly slow.

On Looking Out to Hamsey

A point in the fair distance,
a marker in the land below,
the churchtower silver-grey
above frostpaved river plains.
Village, property, stone. Lanes
turned permanent long ago.

Here, the safe solid structures.
Names, dates, bloodties. Contours,
cracks, places you can step inside.
The rise of things. Insects, last light.
Late trees cast black with height.
What is far, what is near. Hamsey
in the flood plains below.

Ah the wanting gets in the way

I want as little as possible.
I want this poem to be three lines long.
I start this day small.
I am small.
I am a child.
I have a bag of sweets that I tip away.
I keep just a few.

Three Poems

Bukhte Radosti
Bay of Joy
our first trip
up river
we walked back
through pines and smoke
shashlik on the fire
mosquitoes in the air.

Do you remember
the yellow gorse,
red rose hips
on the beach,
November sea?
We looked down
from those cliffs
as we look down
from these days.

You talk to me
I'm behind you
your voice passes
through the wall
of your body
a loss of clarity
recouped in tone.
A sound from the other side –
wait, I'll be there soon.

Notes from No Place

In Canyon it's deeper
down than up. All stops
blocked, all holds barred.
This is dead-end don't
you know. And all the trees
you've ever seen, not here.

In Grit it's all under your
feet, not to say that's a prob.
No probs in Grit. All shuffle
and feel it, perhaps hoping to
one day take a long skid out.

In Day you'll go wherever
it wants to take you. Try
saying left, you won't know
what's hit you. Desire, middling
preference. Slap in the face.

In Wire it's one foot
then another. Whatever's
below is just the endgame.
Think straight ahead. Hands
in pockets. Bravely you go.

In Filament you pull one
thread right out to the end.
Things happen here. It's
violet and all around you
are shreds of dogged ambition.

In Shade it's the setting
of the sun that gets you
so they make it noon all
day. In the square shadows
laugh, glad to be so reduced.

In Petal you think you're as
pretty as. You see no point in
skills, ideas. We know no future
here. We've heard that what
is green rules. We are king.

Family Likeness

We pass at times on others' stairs, perhaps
one day we'll sit and talk. *We're almost twins*
you know, born two generations apart. I'll seek
to break the bond: born on the first of the month
true, both with two brothers, but me in the middle.
Languages, yes, were all we could do but look
at the places they've taken us. *Now ask, now ask.* And I ask:
am I to leave my bones abroad like you?

Your legs, your legs, she'll say, what I'd do for such legs.
The accent's there. Forty years of foreignness
keeping her apart. Walkéd, talkéd, touchéd.
Betrayed by tongue each day. Remember your endings
I'll say – walked, talked, touched, now you.
And what of your children? All right, are they to have
an accent not my own? Be born in a place
not my home? *So you know home is not where you make it?*
Enough now with tempting fate. Just wait, just wait.

Touched

I have not touchéd
she says, sliding a piece
of food from hers to ours.
It makes the rounds,
we refuse, childish squeamish –
what things from under fingernails?
Or perhaps her tongue was there.
A family unlike ours would
drink unthinkingly from
the same glass. We preferred
to keep well apart the pieces
of us that others could touch.

And later we sometimes
joke *I have not touchéd*
and scrape our plates.
Who knows she wanted
to give and to never take.
O, how she gave and was sure
to never take.

Italian Lessons

One year, her last good one,
she wrote out all the verb endings
on a sheet of paper and gave it to me.
Is this all I need to know?
-are, -ere, -ire, -ato, -uto, -ito.
Then she went downhill.
We'd sit in front of her heater
repeating the present perfect.
Now I know the future.

Snowstorm

Thoughts settle
then melt
infinite versions
of themselves
insistent only on their descent
making no sense
no pattern
I am the patch of ground
they couldn't care less
whether they cover.

Outside a car
passes wetly.
I may be some time
yet.

Pull me into pieces

you'll find no minor parts
no place for a centre
each centre is a place

by-ways
       inroads

look inside
what will you find?
Lots of bells
       clattering around.

In/Out

One's in, one's out.
Each pockets the scoop of the other.
In says, when push comes to shove
I'll push, snort, turn like a fish.
Out says, I feel you my quivering friend.
In laughs, o let me alone.
Together they are stumped.
Shifty as a bag of beans.
They roll gathering speed.
Inside are eyes ripening.
Inside are shoots hardening.
In grows out.
New space to fill at will.
Out waits. Palpitates.
Take what you can. There are limits
to this contouring land.
In as yet thinks it can.

Lost Lines

All my life, the distance
Those baroque clouds
How they're painted on
A car skims the asphalt
I can see the gap between the tyres and the road
Those could be cypress trees
This could be Italy
That could be an eagle
One magpie then another
Is this continuation?

Slowly the good weather passes over the next valley
I wish I could filament a thought
but splinter
That bird makes a sound like two stones
clicking together
Wind's at the fence
Bird's flown off now
still clicking
and   and

Indian Summer

Fullness like tides of grass
and conkers popping
creamily from their shells.

Blackberries almost gone now,
rooks caw,
lumber over railway tracks,

and the sun's rays warm
as if remembering when
there was all the time in the world.

Soon a first fire will be lit
and all things living will gather home.

Arrival

By full moon
we'll know
whether or not.

Mother and child
on my desk
all year.

Sweet pea
flowering
into winter.

> Arrival
> sweetest
> never leave.

> > We'll sit here
> > pen in hand
> > head on chest.

> > Virgin's blue
> > wrapped
> > round you.

> > Always
> > your breath
> > pacing mine.

Morning Song

Mornings
your song
is an 'o'
of loveliness,
a bare whisper,
tender of breath
feathering the air.
You fill gently
   to the brim
with dove softness
no-no, no-no,
your self is a petal
freshest of yous
flowering
  newly
in-in, in-in,
now
  come
      hear
  speak
or, or.

Done, in Gold

Soft skinned we are,
light that comes we take,
baby and I attached we lie,
but I must also think.
What comes? A luminous cloud
through the high window
gifted in parts. I make the whole.
It lasts, mixes with itself,
stirs up a gleaming mountain.
I smell the glacial drive
from deserts past.

Dune flowers,
dust flowers
shining in the sun.

Down there I see cheeks
still going strong. We are warm,
alight, all heart, one looking up, one
delved in. With this breath
I'll measure out
the distances
to come. Attached,
unattached,
done.

Notes

p. 9   *yabloko:* apple

p.13   The second verse consists of the names of places and geographical regions that reach across the territory of the former USSR. Vendors bring their honey from these places to the Moscow honey fair.

p.15   *protalina:* a thaw hole that reveals the ground below
        opushka: the edge of the forest

p. 17   *malchik:* boy

p. 19   *Budyonovka:* a hat that was part of the Red Army uniform
        'synthicated': a word made up by the poet

p. 20   *tovarish:* comrade

p. 29   *kokoshnik:* a decorative element in traditional Russian architecture and also the name of a traditional Russian head-dress
        kokoshniki is the plural.

p. 37   *dacha:* a small country house

p. 38   *izba:* log house
        samovar: an urn used to heat and boil water for tea

p. 40   Yasnaya Polyana is the estate of Leo Tolstoy comprising woodland, orchards, meadows, his house and grave.
        lastochka: swallow

p. 51   *shashlik:* skewered meat roasted over wood or charcoal

Caroline Clark

Saying Yes In Russian

"We breathe a sea-thawed air from a sea that isn't there." – Caroline Clark's collection explores the Russia she knows intimately – city, forest, snow – and always with a music that seems to soothe the fear of gaps she finds, edges beyond the edge. Clark's poems have a serenity, a beauty, that knows what perhaps the best lyric knows: "weightlessness takes the strain."

Richard Price, author of *Lucky Day*

In this compelling first collection, Caroline Clark plays with languages and with language itself. Her vision is pure and touched with the numinous. Her poems, delicate yet strong, at times impressionistic, catch different lights, essences, tastes and colours – all laid on carefully with a palette knife. Through time and place she leads the reader to the centre of things in a sure, promising voice totally her own.

W.S. Milne

ISBN 978-1-908527-04-2

Price £8.50 €11 $13